ばかげている

【ミクコンセプト】

思考は思考をもたらす

思考は人生のすべてを支配します

際限なく閉じ込められた

Miku Kumiko

ridiculous 2/2

koans

meditations

thoughts

remarks

ridiculous

Bibliografische Information der Deutschen Nationalbibliothek: Die Deutsche Nationalbibliothek verzeichnet diese Publikation in der Deutschen Nationalbibliografie; detaillierte bibliografische Daten sind im Internet über dnb.dnb.de abrufbar.

【ミクコンセプト】

Herstellung und Verlag:

BoD – Books on Demand, Norderstedt

ISBN: 9783753446202

And the day is already wasted

Everything that is like that cannot even exist. And there is one inside of me. Told me before. We took it and did it well. We ask and begin to have. And no longer take the guesswork out of it. It's not in the ego. Gradually I've wasted myself. I am wide awake and accompany the day. There are no meaningless hours here. Dream and feel a true spirit. Nothing was done. Nothing is what you thought it was. And the day is wasted again.

The end is already near

Tired of worry. We play too well. Belief in
the beginning and the end. Loved deep in
your heart. Justice is most important. Play
with the days. And death comes with you.
The bum itches. Hear a familiar laugh. I
pocket the having. The end is already near.

Or do you have me and are you popular

The pleasure foams away. Love relationships are lost. Bleeding hearts can be seen. Forget about balanced absenteeism. I am trapped in myself and in your thoughts. Pain enchants the day. Feel the end weakly. Good feelings are not always good. Be a better person and choose me. Leading with the lowest instincts is the art. And scream out the pain of life. If you give up I believe. It's a mindful ride. Or do you have me and are you popular?

Find and try

The sun has set, it got cold relatively quickly, the nonchalance faded. A lot came up in the discussions, especially those who were rarely allowed to talk, talked about the warm day and now said very cheeky and didn't really let themselves be pampered. So I listened and pretended wrong and very interested, my ears couldn't open and the brain said curfew. And the sound waves of the otherwise silent ones didn't really reach me. So I could think of anything and I was too lazy to do that. The eternal old rewarmed stories, they reeked of antiquity, there were no new experiences and the pants got tighter and tighter. What a dog, I thought, a smart dog with a mind like a cat and eating like a pig. The beneficiaries consider themselves lucky and really attribute everything to their talents. You have to be confident, train hard and tell yourself how to do it, then you can achieve something. And the know-it-all did not stop, there were simply those who knew and I was and am a failure.

A mistake. Life goes on and thousands of mouthpieces are desperately looking for ears instead of thinking of a brain that processes at least parts. Answers are not wanted, discussions are not necessary, and understanding should be a joke. A dog trying to manipulate me, a bastard who eats like a nervous pig. The brain is bled to death, the greatest story is taken, so please think about it. A well-made lie does nothing in itself, no hurricanes will hit you, and you probably won't notice yourself either. But the tender love in your tense heart is still looking for something, a piece of the coveted happiness.

Everything will be different again and the questions of when to start and will never end. It does not matter. Everything is always new, perceive yourself, no matter how, and you will shine like a fat piece of bacon, look inside yourself with joy and doubt. Find and try.

Look to the near future when you wake
up

I ran at full speed, forgot my stomach and
beamed into tired faces, our togetherness
is encouraged, the good and sensible
upbringing. Aging is no longer important
and the hardened lower legs do not
remain free of varicose veins. Where is the
world going? I'll be there. My hat has a
wide brim and the felt is the finest, I don't
mind the sun and I'm ready for more
humiliations. Look to the near future
when you wake up.

Go home and be the night

The days are over. Once again. Find
meaning in the days of tomorrow. There
is nothing left of the profit. And night fell.
The omniscient gaze grew rigid. The night
brought cool air. The wish was not really
granted. The text was misunderstood. And
there is nothing left to read. So everything
goes in circles. Well called. Everyone
understood. Go home and be the night.

Sure well done

Thrown off track. Look at yourself from a different angle. The benefit remains. Or does that make you happy too? Nobody thinks anymore. Superiority is becoming less and less important. We feel a burn in the back of our head. And we sniff our way through. What else can you show? Kindness and compassion? Do you want to be praised? Call for attention. Always be ready. And be the beloved helper. Sure well done.

Disappear

Understand well and have a clear opinion, ignore the discarded monkeys for a short time, the trodden thoughts do not have to get out of control, tomorrow is another day. We believe in miracles, in miraculous coincidences and in divine chance. The day after tomorrow will bring redemption, take a heart and caress your restlessness, fill your lungs with pure alpine air and look at your life. And like and love the picture and fight like an opinion maker, believe in values and not see crazy monkeys as brothers. We mean that, and we need it very much, and yet we're going to disappear too quickly.

That makes sense

Got lost in the darkness of the principles
of having enough land and gold, and often
standing and waiting. To depend on social
feelings, not to live differently and to kiss
the world just to be tidy. Since the
imagination ran well, we could afford
more than average. Many congratulated us
and cut open our car tires at night.
Understanding well is the basis of
friendship. So I take off my hat and say
hello to everyone, meet friendly faces and
reap great thanks. Thanks for nothing.
Prepare me well for the evening, make a
good soup and take my notebook, read it.
That makes sense.

And sometimes get lost

What is the truth? Did you meet the truth while walking? There is simply nothing left of dirt and shine. The desired answers are more difficult. Always reinvented. Not consciously lied. I don't even know the truth. And sometimes get lost.

Give me a kiss

Obviously I aged quickly without doing
big things, but I still dreamed of the big
day. Nobody can know what's going to
happen to me and maybe to you too. Our
shopping carts were always more than full,
the indomitable ones stand up again and
are nowhere to be seen. The world
responded pretty well to me but never
ordered or asked for anything special.
There is nothing to ask, the expansion of
consciousness does not tickle and who
would like to discover the day with us?
Time goes by almost too slowly; it is
impossible to catch up with yourself. As
always, entrusted secrets are revealed and
the most intimate becomes the joke of the
day. The old also don't bring anything
with them, the young think about the
moment or not at all and teach again and
mop up and don't necessarily want to be
there anymore. Hide well and nobody will
find you, a sadness, a laugh from a
bystander, hope never dies so they say yes.
The horror came with the hangover, the
toilet bowl was too far away and the

hunger is likely to be gone for the near future, and the know-it-all continued to quickly watch over the basics and be quick to joke. I feel sick. Terribly bad. Without strength, there is no point showing off, and the lost spoke weakly of the future. Everything slipped away, you pointed and shook your head. Give me a kiss.

I hear you

Take care of yourself. Do not get
wounded. I don't have a head. For the
many thoughts. You sing a song and fly
through the air. Describe good words. Hit
right in the heart. Attract attention.
There's a lot to hear. Unfortunately, the
ear is closed. Conversations remain. And.
Do you see me? Or I hear you.

Remains

You're already a little crazy, you knead old
wounds and suddenly get up and walk
away, everything has become too much
and self-giving doesn't need discipline, be
proud of it, stir in the dirt at home, curse
your mother and lie with hers thick
ceiling. Open your head and ask what's
going on, the heavy blanket pushes the air
out of you and you stammer about
freedom, the madman becomes more
intense inside you, the sentences longer
and the music before bed sounds good.
Slowly fall asleep with you, the willpower
remains.

Are

The dirty fingernails just don't look good
and think about the thinking and the
cleanliness and can find out about the
future again or there are also opposing
voices in you and you have always been
and always want to give up and give
yourself and are.

You can't change it

The goat is going home. The child is
getting older. The big man is falling apart.
Caresses are exchanged. Accepted and
lost. Greetings and a warm welcome. The
worms are eating their way through your
head. The heavenly song becomes quieter.
Where are they? Are you already sleeping?
You disappear in the dark. Everything
seems calm and lonely. You can't change
it.

And the temple bell rings

I've already had my fill and I'm still hungry for more, my stomach is already full, but my tongue is licking for more. There is something nice about meetings. Grandma is chatting excitedly with other people. Grandma is resting at the cemetery and the boiled beef tastes good as always. The days are coming and the earth will be your final resting place. Maybe then boiled beef and rolls will no longer be eaten and maybe the children will laugh even louder than they do now. Do not be sentimental, there will be nothing left of you and the next ones will need space. And the temple bell rings.

And sometimes you get visited

The day has not started for a long time. At
least I think so. The shoes are pressing on
your toes. They should be one size too
tight. It hurts and distracts me. My face is
turning. And you apologize for your
problems. There is no meeting. Come
here and hug me. It won't do any good,
but it's nice. Make friends and find
something good in life. Time flies quickly.
And you still can't catch anything. Always
hoped. Explore much of the day again.
And sometimes you get visited.

And yet you lose yourself

What would you like to understand, nature's system or your favourite counterpart, or at least you yourself reach into your backpack and take out your snack package. You will find the right pattern and you will not want to do anything with it. Use the trick of different perspectives and slip from one person to another. As if this is your end in itself and you start singing a nice song, showing yourself almost naked and still you get ignored. Then we run off and grab as much luggage as possible to have more with us and are happy to have hoarded. I tie myself up and ask everyone in this tight spot and don't hear anything, but I don't feel uncomfortable. The self seems beautiful and believes again in the higher, like everyone else, and in understanding and happiness. And yet you lose yourself.

And you are dead

Got suffocated. The skin becomes cold.
The tip of the nose slowly turning blue.
The day tasted sweet. Love gives itself to
me. Can't take anything anymore. And
have a hard time having an opinion. The
smell becomes penetrating. A shudder
goes obliquely over the observer.
Opinions come to life. The sweat tastes
disgusting. And you are dead.

Too deep

After many conversations, I fell asleep and tried to come to terms with the new truths. I wanted to say something too, but nobody listened or said anything about my opinion. The deep sleep recovered me and the voices became quieter, actually I didn't understand anything, but I still wanted to talk to you and be there. Many sentences were said, especially about the right behaviour to better understand others. I also felt sick from the bottom up, from the wet lips and the skewer flying through the air. Cant care for the kindness I was hoping for, sleep is the best cure. Take a swig of poison, I feel sick, and take a kind, deep look at the word pile. Too deep.

Sense

Finally, a thought with meaning arises,
very brief and quiet, flee and empty the
mind and breathe deeply and give life an
artificial meaning.

All holiness disappears in prayer

The piano is booming in the neighbouring
apartment. The neighbours turn up their
voices. Discussions are fuelled. If you
have strong feelings, you belong in it. Let
yourself be celebrated and you will be a
hero. Look at all the faces and say yes.
The next day will come. And happiness
can be small again. You give yourself a
new day. All holiness disappears in prayer.

To let

When I fall over and gasp for air in the
ground, briefly discuss but somehow not
be heard, my mouth chews wet mud, the
day sounds joyful in my heart and lying
down suits me, my fingers drill holes in
the ground and the day is now done.

Rapture and slip

The chest feels constricted, some things
haven't been cleared up and are spreading
from the stomach to the throat, there will
be a beginning again and I will treat myself
to an ice cream. Greetings are no longer
my habit, dialogues leave a bad taste and
yet I become more relaxed. My ulterior
motives are drowning in the swamp of the
many prospects, but I still lick the ice
cream with relish and wonder if the fear
will lessen. Tomorrow maybe you can take
a deep breath and make new life plans.
Rapture and slip.

The farewell is particularly comforting

I ran around shouting funny sayings to my colleagues, posture eased a bit, walking makes you tired. Nobody will see if the oven is still on or already off, but it will definitely be hotter. I was still listening and was amazed at the well-rhymed statements and harsh sayings. My stomach growled and hunger dominated my head. This is how the madness should begin, important things in the environment and one small dominant thing. A good start in this environment. The farewell is particularly comforting.

Everything makes sense

The ear was clogged with the many words.
Mouths move towards you. Don't know
about tomorrow. The affection is also an
affection. Get up again. Everything makes
sense.

And we keep looking

We have everything new locked in our hearts. Come here and find my happiness. I am happy to give you a piece. You were looked after for many hours and you were hungry. I won't be full today. There is no end to thirst either. We humans let off steam. Thunderstorms don't irritate us. The nose was hit bloody. And the screaming gets on our nerves. All friends were lost. And we keep looking.

Future

Be against it and come up with a good
sentence and announce it without feeling
scared and slowly wake up and float into a
sweet future.

And go when you want

Exciting compulsions. Don't be bad to yourself. Everything was recorded in secret. I answered. Danger. Nothing gets worse. It is. And go when you want.

The beginning has been made again

Sit up and see better. Don't be alone
anymore. Greet and perceive. Eyes meet
eyes. A quick hug. A tear fertilizes the
earth. Be noticed. The beginning has been
made again.

Be

Being spoiled by being, I often confess
appearances and make new plans, there is
a mountain that I will climb and then I
will understand myself or not and I am
here and I rub the dirt out of the spaces
between my toes and I am happy.

The nest is empty

You lie frozen in the trickle and count
your fingers, everyone is there and you
look tired. The night was cold, the
encounters were unsuccessful and the
spirit of wine weighed on you, there
wasn't much to say. Really enjoyed it and
be proud of it, really drank and be proud
of it. Proud, very proud and happy. Well-
coordinated days judge us and find the
freedom so good to drink and eat and be a
pig. The relationships that please and the
big gulp, the right to stay, make you loyal.
Religious finders of meaning break up and
bite their nails, commands that must be
obeyed, and laugh for the rest of the day.
Staggering home coldly and looking for
the door key. The nest is empty.

The singing sounds high

Your leg was peed on by the dog. The
downpipe is hanging heavily. The wet
takes the cold with it. Your nonchalance
crumbles quickly. The leg becomes less
important. Run against your wall. And you
hit your nose bloody. Every beginning is
difficult. The pants dry slowly. And slowly
the blood on the face dries. The
conversations are getting louder again.
Everyone come together. And talk wildly
to each other. The past disappears. The
singing sounds high.

Be deactivated

Chopped off spinning mills are in the bowl for everyday eating. The vanity grows rampant and produces thick ulcers, the sun grills the brown raised facial contours black. It gets cold on the back where no one can look, and all questions are answered quickly, nothing is owed, everything depends on a good opinion or you firmly believe in a good opinion. You don't have to close your heart, be ready for all feelings, because I want to say that I live and also stumble. But be vain and get blackened and take a deep breath. Spit the mucus out of the lungs, everything is not what we thought. Deactivated.

How well can you wait

Spit on the face. Cake sticks to the
buttocks. I yodelled and smiled at you. We
are fraternizing quickly now. Time has
done it to us. Who is going to be angry?
How are you? How well can you wait?

Days and evenings die off

We will see. What will make us happy? Do you want to take a deep breath again someday? Drugs dampen us. Nothing that can be lost. Everything stays the same. We meet in neutral rooms. Wake up and be mine. There is nothing to understand. Clear all times. Days and evenings die off.

Entangled

The drunkards join forces and have come
up with new slogans, want to create
insecurity, are in the right place and take
everything with them and know no mercy,
crazy and normal and entangled.

What is it then

Have a good idea of the beautiful, first
and foremost tall and slim and then funny
and nice and then young and nondescript
and best heard. The swamp concerns us
all, he said, and it's still stuck. The good
character was quickly forgotten and so
was the strong personality that this
character became. Suck in the leaden air
and nod stubbornly, the index finger
belongs in the holster and you look at the
name. What is it then?

There is no mercy

To be warmly present with opinions, to
shout apart is something easy and I know
you. The counterpart becomes terrifyingly
large and there is no mercy, everyone
drinks. The rain is part of it, silence is the
main part of the mood, beautiful and ugly,
that's good. A catchy tune spreads
endlessly in the head. There is no mercy.

Or at least it goes on

A considerably large mind does not give
up. Does not tease other fine spirits.
Listening is a courtesy. To be gone soon.
Find the good hour. What do you have to
ask? Don't lose your counterpart.
Otherwise they close. Or at least it goes
on.

And abdicate at some point

My sore feet need a bath. The cornea
becomes softer. Take a deep breath and
experience it all over again. Nothing is
free and you have to pay. Take care of the
slowly dying body with sensitivity. I am
waiting for you and you will not come.
And the freedom that is believed in does
not exist. Still believe in it. And grow old
in the process. The feet are slowly
becoming wrinkled. The heat goes to my
head. I haven't been happy for a long
time. Friends ring my doorbell. I am not
listening and my feet are dissolving.
Confidence is lost. The whole of being
collapses. Even strong thoughts are no
longer helpful. And in the end you have
fun. And abdicate at some point.

A fertile mind

The weeds and the lettuce are springing
up, we've added enough fertilizer and
we're ready for anything. The cramp in the
left side of your face is slowly subsiding,
you may have accidentally sucked on the
fertilizer and you get sick as a result.
That's how it is to play with the rich
harvest, not everything is always perfect,
wanting more is the basis. Look at the
field growing wild. Massage the almost
dead half of your face well and start a
discussion with the holistic thinkers. They
buy into you and want to see interest and
you should quickly give up your good
face. Win and lose faster, you can get a
cramp in the other half of your face or in
your heart, but do not destroy yourself
completely or you will not be able to pay
interest. And belief in everyday life
disappears quickly, you don't know the
past either, business matters and the good
luck charm is the fertilizer. Strengthen
your life and find new network partners,
help each other, life brings indescribable

profit and small pains will be bearable. A
fertile mind.

Out

I didn't dare say anything and I hid and
enjoyed my life, sniffing my own stench
over and over again. Maybe bliss is there,
go back again, right into the darkest hole,
count off my thoughts and live it out.

Find

Use words to play sloppy and manipulate
the vulnerable and catch you and use
words to find hope for the glorious future.

Or have you already become perfect

Wake up briefly at night, look at the alarm clock and see a time that you will soon forget. The unexplained problems of the day are twitching in the muscles, there is no longer any need to think through, you like the fast-paced world and do it quite well in terms of success. You can compare the few unknown dark figures with yourself and your own will certainly be examined intensively. You can have a say at any time and have a quick answer ready. Forget your gaps, from tomorrow you won't have any more and you are no longer here in the world but under the earth. Or have you already become perfect?

Because the rest is appropriate there

The ghosts have flown out. I stand all alone in the house. The dark sky does not show the stars. And the illusions show up stronger. One ghost remained. And he's afraid of reality. Only nobody knows the reality. And is always new. Ghost hands grab and touch. The upper eyelid begins to twitch vigorously. One tic and you've won. Because the rest is appropriate there.

Die slowly

Accept and press. Push into a corner. Be
especially unfree. Got it again forever. We
don't see you. It stays forever. And it's
filled with worry. Give me the opinion. Or
do you stay alone. It doesn't help you.
Talking to you. Teach you. And then hide.
Die slowly.

The stomach growls

It itches in the ear, ear wax is looking for
its way into the open air, the premonitions
of the wonderful festival brought the little
heart a bit of luck. Make up a personality
and reinvent that authority and everything.
So you will survive and positive thinking
will take over when depression or anxiety
arise, forget them, life is ruled by the spirit
no matter which direction. Or not. The
stomach growls.

And a new beginning

The cold doesn't give in. The snot runs
down the upper lip into the mouth.
Otherwise there was nothing. We will see.
A friendliness says hello. You haven't
discussed the highest point yet. The
sufferings in the cross plague again. And
the biting doesn't get any better. Good
things come back. Old illnesses just stick.
There are no limits in your head. Or is the
space shrinking every day. The friendly
employee is proud. And a new beginning.

And respect decreases

The mown meadow lay there like fur,
when you lay down you had the feeling of
being safe, the insects rested, the ticks
took a nap in the afternoon. Sharp
observers had a break from the radio and
the sun was shining beautifully, everyone
was unprotected, the day was bearable.
The fellow travellers showed the best side
and made themselves smaller,
complimented us with soft faces and still
said that we are poor worms. Regardless,
but oddly, no one should really want envy,
especially the poor and the lost. Put my
hand in my pocket and try to stand there
casually, the pants are too loose and look
very cheap. Throwing a saying into the
crowd allows you to belong, sit down with
your legs apart and show an obvious
untouchability. Nothing works. And
respect decreases.

And hopefully you dissolve

The track has been deleted. The insects
are buzzing around crazy. There is no rest.
And swallow a fly. It's not satisfactory.
And that's why there is nothing to tell. An
uncomfortable feeling gets stuck in the
throat. The tongue feels furry. The fly
continues to hum in the stomach. And I'm
thirsty for alcohol. Memories fly towards
me. The summer will be hot. Insects
thicken the air. And seek refuge with your
mouth open. Everything is well thought
out. Swallow quickly and forget about the
bite. The head is still white. And hopefully
you dissolve.

What a sentence

Great flashes of thought list your view of life, are related to all human beings, and have spoken to yourself. The feeling cannot be different or at least the imagination is good because I argue with myself and love doesn't know each other and you drown in the sunset. What a sentence.

Or even old age

Have knocked good sayings. Well learned
from books and often heard too. You can
do a lot. And in the end nothing remains.
Maybe a good saying on the tombstone.
Or a hint from someone. Collect a lot and
build an altar. Seeking allies in madness.
And bless the places of worship. Who are
your friends? Where will they go with you?
Will they love you and love each other?
Or do they just think with you? The beard
is long and very old. Everything has to be
right and you will find yourself. Or not
find it. The golden heart should not be
weighed. The time stands still. Everything
has a name, which makes it look good.
With or without it doesn't matter. It is the
young morning. Or even old age.

Buttoned

Well drunk looking for a brightness in the
head and I keep looking and find an
opulent piece of soft mass and scare and
feel a stinging in the stomach area and see
holes already eroded, reach deeper and
deeper and find a flexible law that is well
dressed and very buttoned up.

Alone now

Simple conversations ripple along,
willingly admit the opinions of the others
and laugh inwardly about it, the fear will
come soon enough. Take it easy and you
will get well, the discussions become more
profound and everyone forget each other.
The heart beats restlessly, the psyche
triggers the descent and the disease begins
to germinate. And I got sick and the birds
chirp a love song and attract the females.
Pretended states confuse the audience, the
player doesn't know what to do and quick
thoughts almost make you crazy. Know
yes, but the knowledge is pure theory
because everything, as we already know,
was reinvented. Clouds pull in at the
speed of an express train, blacken the sky
and wait for the great discharge, self-pity
needs nourishment and can be found
everywhere. The nasal congestion begins
to run, everything becomes easier and the
interlocutors disappeared. Alone now.

And I didn't think of anything more for the day

Hug me lightly and smell me. Your hand feels very wrinkled. The goal should be found. And the proverbs will come to an end. Or it will never end. Good friends take my responsibility away from me. Prefer them. And say goodbye quickly after your job is done. Soon you will no longer have a will of your own. Finding this is a great art in itself. Air your ears and find peace. Feel bled out and without a fresh start. It all started somewhere. Maybe read a good book. I didn't laugh about it. And I didn't think of anything more for the day.

And watch out

I've always been afraid. Back then in war
and now in war. Everyone likes to
celebrate parties. You and me and without
big questions. The big breakthrough
comes. Or just breaks through. The big
community. With countless dependencies.
Come with me. And soak up everything.
And watch out.

The day ends

A red moon goes with me. Illuminated
and very close. There is still an unpaid bill.
It's slowly getting dark inside of me. There
is nothing to take. We can understand
together. The hours are lost. The day
ends.

Night

Fresh cool air pours into the night, cools
our heads and we believe we can see
better now, but it doesn't work, nothing
should get better with a fight and the
coolness is good, take a quick look and fall
in the middle the night.

Thanks and amen

My love is great. The pump is currently
pumping. Everything pulsates. The wind
whistles through your pants. My forehead
is burning. Many adventures have passed.
Talk to yourself, does the conversation
sound friendly? People blink at the sky
and laugh. A wonderful day. Troubling
confidence. Did you get closer to you?
Thanks and amen.

But that's good

The beard grows on my face, looks terrible, and I feel bad. Life hangs by a thread. Love and the tender find pity, although it brings something, shortly before the breakup, shortly before the crash. Perhaps. The day works well with everything around. I lean against the neighbour and tell about solutions that have not been found, he doesn't listen. But that's good.

Maybe eat too

Stay in trouble. Knowledge is a way. Be
especially lonely. The belief in finding
remains. Don't let anything get worse.
And blame. Questions pass. Requests
remain. Hope is good. Eat the jelly. Maybe
eat too.

All conversations in the head are free

Come from the dark corner. The taste in the mouth feels bad again. Take a deep breath and start coughing. The neck pain will subside one day. Hasn't anyone been looking for you in years? Are you still at the beginning or do you know more? It won't do you any good either way. Just take your life and you will want a lot. Start talking and really without big stories. And it's up to you again. All conversations in the head are free.

Or not

Preach the truth without exception.
Receive truth and read it down to the
fictional detail. Give everything for the
best. Blame and free the guilt. Getting
fatter and smelling bad too. The sun is
burning the earth is dry. Everyone
becomes more alert and friendlier.
Contact everything. And you are accepted.
You can tell others later. Life has good
taste. And the givers receive you. To
appreciate successful relationships and to
be wrong. Show your lips and become
even friendlier. Understand you.
Understand me. Or not.

But the head has a hole

My daily game of material stakes never ended and never brought luck, why should it? But be happy and you want too much or nothing more. The word love cannot really be used there. The days went by and my heart grew weaker, a restless life with no real challenges. The great challengers sat bitterly on their park benches and commanded the world, stole its essence, and were quickly eliminated. Sneak on tiptoe into the homeless privacy and they will really study what they have what I don't. Is my roof over my mind the panacea or is it starting to crumble? I think my head is wet from acid rain. The hair sticks together greasily and the last few days have not been wonderful, nothing comes back and the memory doesn't really bring much. Take a deep breath and place again, the highest and the last bet and you lose. But the head has a hole.

Summer is already here

Look relaxed into the sun's rays. It's warm
and the day is good. You keep getting
thirstier. And I take a deep breath. Reach
into what I have. And buy some news.
Found a lot. The future is none of our
business. The songs get quieter. It's hot
and I can barely breathe. Did you break
out? And I scream with happiness.
Summer is already here.

You are just

The little man comes and takes his ego
away, becomes a little kid and puts the
knowledge up his ass, it doesn't matter,
cuddling is never free and the music
sounds harsh. You are just.

An eternal repetition

The cookies taste very sweet. My heart is beating very wildly again. I missed the intersection again. The old people now have nothing more to say. The new thing tastes very worn. The calves got stronger and stronger. But overall I was getting more tired. I still have hope. And that has to do with enjoyment again. When will the deep philosophy finally come? When does wisdom come to us? When does enlightenment come? An eternal repetition.

Or everything will be fine

The lump was easy to pinch out, it quickly turned into massive inflammation and the face could no longer be shown. Give me a kiss and don't haunt me with visions of the future, the evening looks cool and the TV shows show boring discussions. When I get closer and don't feel at home today, my nose is blocked and my bald head reflects the rest of the world. Disgusting. We believe in a better future, read smart books about the street and fall asleep with a headache. A little luck lies in the fridge and has an expiration date. Come here and give me the remote, I'll change channels and believe again. The angels smile at me friendly and my fat belly hangs heavily between the chair legs. Or everything will be fine.

And run in circles

We shake hands. Congratulations and thank you very much. Hand placed on the winner's shoulder. And the heart contracts. Maybe tomorrow everything will be better. We're really contributing to that directly. Everyone should like us. The opponents will press against the wall and laugh. And they spray innocence with blood. We laugh at each other. And run in circles.

The backpack just gets heavier

The right half of the face hung limply, at
first it hurt like hell, then it twitched and
now it no longer gives any sign of life.
Having something massive on your face is
not funny. Everyone can see it and talk,
laugh or make fun of it. The face can be
beautiful; it can be ugly or it can be
disturbed. And you open the vastness of
your soul and you can no longer hide.
Can't hide, tear you down. The backpack
just gets heavier.

Good sentences are not lost

The dearest loved one moved through the country. Your dress fluttered around your head. The underpants that didn't fit could be seen. Go home and clear your throat. Weight your thoughts and sometimes lie. You will be gone soon. You played well and got known. Prepare for the next phase. Become lonelier and patient. Good sentences are not lost.

Delivered new

Wonderful taste. Breathe unsaturated.
Borrowed thoughts. Delivered feelings.
Tongues bitten off. Growing desire. A
short laugh. Felt bad. Shortened way.
Sweet taste. Crooked fingers. Healing
prayers. Well adjusted. Fell down gently.
Delivered new.

And nothing else

Gnarled fingers grip. The Buddha shines brightly. I am careful. Immerse yourself in the pseudo-reality. Another world is being born. Modern wood smells pleasant. Be at home. And nothing else.

The toilet paper is used up

I felt involved, familiar and accepted, the opinions were well received, everyone agreed with me and the stench creeps out between the cracks in the door. The principles sound good and I can't really tell if I've had enough, this requires concepts, records and comparisons. I'm too lazy and unhappy for that right now. The spiritual things come and the world is almost infinitely full of words, how does it work? Keep the latest news in mind and be easy to find new ideas. Have a good idea for the future and reach everywhere. The toilet paper is used up.

And the rule was broken again

Come here now and don't lift your leg.
Inquiries are welcome. Beautiful voices
call for the neighbour. Have swallowed
well. Don't be aggressive and meet up
with others again. The old fish tastes
terrible. And not recognize your own
neuroses. You have pulled out and
smeared everything important. Happiness
dissolves. And go back to the
neighbourhood. Take a round and despise
yourself. Calm down and swallow
everything. Short inquiries are charming.
Say it well. And get dressed well and get
out of here. Spit out the smart sentences.
Party and dance. And the rule was broken
again.

Laughed briefly

The silence in the beginning. Well seen.
Well aimed. Break rules. Insight. A
theatre. Without. And at the beginning.
And good. Everything else. No ifs. The
ease. No thoughts. Old man. Also a start.
Laughed briefly.

And you have the sleep

My sleeping fingers want to reach for the switch on the bedside lamp, it doesn't work, they are tight and feel like an even mass of meat. What's next, with no fingers, no hands, I can't find the switch and I can't operate it. In short, is this the end or just the beginning of madness. I hope to go back to sleep and wake up fresh and alert, nowhere else but in the hospital. Quickly answer an important question for me and put my two lumps of meat under my neck. And you have the sleep.

Anyway and done

The pressure in the back of the head has
increased. There are no clear thoughts.
Life in the famous now is now possible.
It's just not convenient. An iron hand
moves my brain. And the butterflies
flutter excitedly. Do you want peace?
Blessed peace and no noise. Get up and
throw the world up. Repetitions are
comfortable. Find it. The deep joy or
happiness. You have no time. Anyway and
done.

And yet everything is fine again

The neighbour greets me warmly and smiles at me, he looks very real and particularly friendly. We talk about the old day and examine the future, hope for peace and continue to enjoy the world of abundance because it is good for us. The garden has been ploughed and looks wild and untidy. Weeds that have grown back will soon cover everything again. And yet everything is fine again.

Pay

Have thought and asked nothing without
actually saying something or even paying.

An insatiable worm fights its way through

Get a kick in the ass. The humiliation eats
a hole in your head. You become a
potential murderer. And forget about all
of your well-intentioned thoughts and
donations for a better life. Your red head
becomes redder. The ego inflates. An
insatiable worm fights its way through.

There is enough to look forward to

The nose is crooked. The neck looks tight.
The corners of the mouth are drawn up.
And everyone is happy. A hustle and
bustle. You meet smiling, abandoned
faces. You can ask. Who can play with the
ball now. It's not a big puzzle. You will
solve it in peace. Not a good start. But a
grandiose ending with an obituary. Do not
run away. Everyone became happy. Fall in
love with a piece of the world. Do not
judge the silence within you. The bustle
goes on. There is enough to look forward
to.

At least for a couple of days

The sour sweets taste perfect, I chew on them and make a new plan. Since summer is already here, I can let out the cold and think about autumn again, about all the joys, the bloodsuckers, the ticks and the taste of the sweets. Make my opinion count, count everything and try to accept the other opinions, especially the beautiful and loving and holistic opinions, they should not be radical, it is scary. Take my favourite game and distract myself, my mouth is always filled with sweet and sour candy, the blood sucking has not yet arrived and I quickly ask myself a few more questions. Then feel good again, not often. At least for a few days.

Sing a song

I've built a world for myself. This idea
goes well with my skill. The shoes shine
polished. Read the books carefully. Eyes
wide open. And the day adapts to the
thought. Let's sing happy songs. We
belong together and network. Everyone is
proud to have the other as a friend. The
nose is blocked and we sound nasal.
Come on let's prepare the way. Let the
penultimate day begin. Sing a song.

Have fallen well

I ran quickly through the tunnel, my pants
got wet and dirty from deep puddles,
behind me a hunch and a laughing devil.
Rush and flee, be on your feet and make
sure not to give up. Whistle a song, it
should be a traveling song, and so it
happened that I didn't really do anything
about the devil. Have fallen well.

Get lost in feelings

Have found good words in the book. The
words make sense. And think about a next
step in meaning. To forget the words too
quickly. It is buzzing in the stomach.
Lunch comes out of the mouth. The
words float away. Get lost in feelings.

Captured

The taste is reminiscent of something, the pain in the stomach is not good, the love affairs are in the book, the imagination has caught us.

And nodded

The chants grew louder and more
beautiful. There wasn't a word to
understand. Pressed my lips together
tightly. And looked out of my existence as
skilfully as possible. Innocent. I felt. It's a
great opportunity. And nodded.

A real nod

I nodded diligently to you. And you saw
that casually. Waved busily when he
nodded. Lick your saliva. And nod off. A
real nod.

Dependent

Moved out to get to know the world,
greeted many people, had meaningful
conversations, the taste is sweet and I am
dependent on it.

The pleasure disappears

A beautiful song sounds on the radio. The head wobbles rhythmically. The coffee cools down in the cup. The conversations have stopped. The saliva in the mouth tastes horrible. The pleasure disappears.

Some things are good

The soles of my feet are burning from
running around, I haven't found anything,
but I was able to sweat well and my crotch
increased from day to day. No more
waiting, just march off, reduce your
strength. A few days of hiking will still
come, and yet the restlessness remains
deep in the stomach and works non-stop.
Some things are good.

Have swallowed well

It's thick in the throat. The palate swells.
Tried to be friendly, it all passed. And the
pleasure is not hidden. I hid briefly.
Massaged my toes. Take a deep breath.
Lose the imagination. Have swallowed
well.

And fall asleep

Serious threats affect me. Do you have the strength in you? Teach me again. I forgot too much. I have swallowed me. The cough is good. And fall asleep.

Wind up the daydreams and then go out

My first impressions after waking up were not good, I slept too long, lay too crooked, violent dreams did the usual. I complained again to the wrong person, to myself, and again the self-talk didn't end very soon. When we talk to our heads we all know, heart palpitations, and some days we almost kill ourselves. And the relationship to reality becomes more difficult or not more difficult. What kind of reality do I mean today and again collect a garbage and stick with it. What kind of dreams do you have? And looking for your life balance will be enough for the next few days. Wind up the daydreams and then go out.

Extinguished

Listening in dismay. And don't say
anything about it. Everything sounds like
falling apart. Brains start hanging around.
Just don't be kind. Don't be the first.
Keep calm and cool and appear tired. The
life switches will be found. Do not incite
anything. And everything collapses. Then
feel good. Switched on. Or. Extinguished.

Really

Kisses taste sweet, the gum has already
been chewed and will soon be swallowed,
swallowed well, at night the nightmares
come back and the kisses disappear,
nothing is real.

Fart

A good adventure is worth gold and is
needed, like union with God or
something. Rifle out, put your hands in
your arms and laugh out loud and run into
the nearest face. At some point they will
capture you and treat your laugh and find
an unsolvable problem, the famous one.
The day offers a lot, engine noises,
screaming, partying as well as bread and
games. Discussions about nothing interest
me, sometimes I yell along and yesterday I
cough over them. The lush green of the
grass has a calming effect on the nervous
mind, fear of death only returns at night.
Dear home, protect me and, for my sake,
protect our children too. There is still a
little way to go and we can suppress
anything, even the slightest fart.

Now the now is no longer good

We have been used well. Our feelings
should be right. I organized myself well. I
can't say another word. Marvel and be
amazed. Nothing remains. Thoughts
blink. Hatred became a strong feeling.
Good or not good cannot be said. Shake
my hand while you grip tight. Laugh
heartily. Now the now is no longer good.

It often comes to a quick end

Sitting at home and not feeling alone, waiting for the intruder and working on tough statements is part of it too. It creaks and suddenly it bangs, be ready to jump and hold onto the intended meaning, fear plays a major role. The house becomes a scene; the drama is nearing its climax. I've made enough money and I want to get it in the right channels, sow it and grow a lush plant. I've been eaten up by my own feelings, thoughts have connected, and the world is no longer there. We distribute eternity very selflessly and trust that we will do everything. It often comes to a quick end.

And it comes to an end

The knowledge is not enough. Changes purify the blood. The weeds sprout even on hot days. It's better to party than go to school. This is the world and you are human. And grief comes soon enough. What do we know more today? The old are not getting any younger. Wear and tear brings you to a standstill. And everything sounds good. Friendly and nice. The sun pulls on the flowers. The blaze of colour makes you perk up. You are seen. Life is good. And comes to an end.

The beginning has been made

Look angrily at the tightness. My hate is in my stomach and grunts. You can no longer hear what is being whispered. My eyes went red with crying and my mouth laughed crookedly. The air becomes cooler and more humid. Stick to it mindlessly. The beginning has been made.

The heart calms down

Be available. The environment accepts
you. Eliminate risky actions. Take care of
my laughter. Have you treated yourself
well? Creep into the romantic world. Take
a deep breath in the moist air. The heart
calms down.

Or lose

Seen again and again. Evaluated events.
Take a quick breath in fear for a moment.
The kids are bad. The beginning becomes
more and more difficult. Playful children
fall asleep. The uncertainty is spreading.
And you always start over. Or lose.

In any case

The future is made up of a lot of
conversation and opinions and believing
that we are getting closer, then thinking
and falling asleep. Dreams begin and
purify the past. There can also be good
days, good days in the sun, and good days
in the lap of an illusion. Dream about the
day for a moment and wake up with a sore
throat and believe. In any case.

And

Come out of a good contemplation, pour
deep into yourself, I haven't felt the day
for a long time. The lightness decreases
with me, drives away and grows together,
turns away and disappears. And.

You are something

The suitcase is parked in the cellar, it was
a stressful week, the journeys are
becoming more frequent and you cannot
clarify anything, not even process it, and
certainly not answer. Looking for a deep
conversation. Then be gone again, this
time without a suitcase and without
friendliness. The desperate attempt in the
alley across the street to find the solution
to the sadness may fail, you may fail
everywhere and always. Look at your own
feelings and notice the aching stomach,
but again, be kind and smile and put your
hands in your pockets and start showing
yourself. What kind of role do you like to
have, are you funny and seemingly
carefree, do you seem easy to deal with
everyday life? Or are you the serious one,
the tough one who always smokes cigars
and says nothing? But draw the gun
quickly. Who do you want to be? The
athlete's foot does not go away, itches, and
has a strange colour of skin. The cigar has
smoked and the stomach still hurts. You
are something.

From the good hours

Hurry to the end. There should have been
no birth. The idiots live well. The
appearance looks lively. Believe in stories.
From the good hours.

Take everything with you and unite

Sweet tasting cotton candy covers you. Lie on your back and stare into the beautiful blue of the sky. The world is whole and good. Fall asleep and dream of wild adventures. Car horns build up in the dream and disturb. The story takes a new direction. A thousand impressions narrow. Take it all with you and unite.

It remains a hit

The sun is shining, the day was good, people are sweating and the ice cream seller was making money. I like to repeat my sentences, memorize some guiding principles, and be melancholy criticism. I bought an ice cream, my favourite flavours were silence and melancholy. But for that I only got the devotion and the superstition, or was it some kind of belief? And the sun is shining and the ice is cooling me down. Life is good for me. It stays a hit.

And tomorrow it will come again

Found together compulsively and laughed.
Everything is complex and simple at the
same time. When will we meet again?
Pamper yourself and drink yourself
unconscious. Senseless brotherhoods.
We'll admit a lot more. Nobody will be
interested. The laughter subsides. And
tomorrow comes again.

Heavy

The work brought nothing but wages,
those around you caressed the brave and
nobody valued you, the path remains the
same, the stones are heavy.

Then the day would be perfect

My shirt is drenched in sweat and feels
old, I meet friendly fellow travelers and
talk about the last few days, they about the
last few years and we meet. It is a spell to
be alone, the spell fades with the headache
and dies with death. Dress up well and let
me say hello, be proud of a lot. Proud of
the conquered mountain, of the good
location and of the eloquence. We strut
along and like to stretch out our hands to
the poor and the weak. We are polite and
have good style, we don't lose our tone
and we don't show excitement. Air your
hat, take off your sweaty shirt, shower,
and freshen up. A sublime day, an
important, very important little thing is
still missing. Then the day would be
perfect.

I promise it

Close your eyes and open your heart. I felt
the magic. The toes are shining in the sun.
The taste in the mouth feels better. The
wind blows through the armpits. The
battle was not fought happily. And still
smile. Secretly and ashamed. Throw me
on the grass. Nothing was promised. I
promise it.

Where is the final

Rethink the day late at night. Smell the leaf and take a deep breath. Slip into another dimension. Hear a high, comfortable tone. Cough briefly and spit out the mucus. Smoked too much. Forget what's covered. Let the soul be. Where is the final?

Dancer

I asked the dead fish's slightly squeezed
fisheye how this was done. Look at
yourself and do you feel good, who are
you in yourself, a fisherman or are you a
dancer?

And why don't you admit yourself

The thoughts are slowly drowning. The teeth have already fallen out. Confused conversations with the noise next to you. We are all about to die. And eagerly strive for sentimentality. The last song is tuned. Nobody wants to start right. And why don't you admit yourself?

Why not

My heart weighs heavy. The air is thin.
The breath catches. Children laugh. Time
goes by considerably faster. The
premonition became a certainty. And
that's wrong. All ideas are to be forgotten,
bear nothing. I turn on the light; the room
becomes pleasantly bright. Why not?

これが最後のページです

言うことは何も残っていません

私が言えることはすべて
延々と言われてきました

思考は思考をもたらす
最後の考えが魂と共に逃げるまで

その後、すべてが無料で純粋です

DAVID FÜHRT

DER
SCHLAFWANDLER
Seine Träume sind tödlich

sowie
2 Bonus-Storys

Kurzthrillerband